D1223927

Travelers in Time

ASIA IN THE NINETEENTH CENTURY

A BOOK OF POSTCARDS FROM **THE ROYAL PHOTOGRAPHIC SOCIETY**

POMEGRANATE ARTBOOKS • SAN FRANCISCO

Pomegranate Artbooks
Box 6099
Rohnert Park, CA 94927

Pomegranate Europe Ltd.
Fullbridge House, Fullbridge
Maldon, Essex CM9 7LE
England

ISBN 0-87654-492-8
Pomegranate Catalog No. A791

Pomegranate publishes books of
postcards on a wide range of subjects.
Please write to the publisher for more information.

By the early 1870s, there was practically no corner of Asia that had not been documented by British photographers. An explosion in travel, topographical, and "exotic" photography coincided with the opening in 1860 of the Far East, an area of acute artistic and cultural interest for the British since the China mania of George IV in the early 1800s. Imported Orientalist art, ceramics, textiles, and furniture had created an unreal and supposed familiarity with Eastern countries and peoples. The British were eager to see the landscapes, architecture, and peoples of these highly advanced cultures, and now photographers such as Roger Fenton, Samuel Bourne, John Thomson, and others were able to move in and document the real thing. Although they tended to impose a British pictorial interpretation on their subjects, their determination and commitment must be admired. The empire on which the sun never set presented an awesome challenge to photographers, who worked with large plate glass negatives, heavy and cumbersome equipment, and a variety of unstable chemicals that boiled in the tropical heat and froze in the Himalayan cold.

Roger Fenton (1819–1869), founder of The Royal Photographic Society and its first secretary, accompanied the civil engineer Charles Vignoles to Russia in 1852 to photograph a bridge Vignoles was building across the Dneiper. Finding Moscow's exotic Oriental architecture more appealing than rivers and bridges, Fenton photographed there and then moved on to St. Petersburg and Kiev, becoming the first British photographer to document Russia. His later photographs of the Crimean War (1855) and a series of Orientalist figure studies (1858) show his continuing profound fascination with Russia.

Eighteen-year-old Walter Bentley Woodbury (1834–1885) sailed to Australia in 1852 to make his fortune in the gold fields. Too late for the gold boom, Woodbury turned his hand to photography, opening studios in Melbourne and Java. From his studio in Batavia he made trips to more remote areas, photographed princes, temples "equaling in beauty the largest temples of Nineveh," and exotic scenery and peoples, and sold copies to European merchants trading from Java.

Captain Linnaeus Tripe (1822–1902) was a government photographer employed to document

Southern Indian (1856–1860) and Burmese (1855, 1869–1872) archaeological remains before they decayed further. His photographs—stunning large-format contact prints from paper negatives, waxed for translucency in printing—were published in six volumes.

Samuel Bourne (1834–1912) was perhaps the most intrepid of the new breed of explorer-photographer. He abandoned a banking career in Nottingham to follow his passion for photography in India. From 1862 to 1869 he made photographic treks through the Himalayas and Kashmir, often under appalling conditions, and relayed his experiences in a series of articles in the British Journal of Photography. Bourne also sold copies of his photographs to British military and government employees stationed in India during the period of the British Raj.

Felice Beato (1825–1903) traveled all over Asia, photographing the aftermath of the Indian Mutiny and the Chinese Opium Wars as well as more topographical, tourist-oriented scenes. Among his most successful photographs are exquisite hand-colored portraits of ordinary working people in Japan in the 1860s.

John Thomson (1837–1921) traveled and photographed in the Far East for ten years and published illustrated books of his journeys. His photographs of China in particular convey his sense of wonder and enthusiasm for that country's sights and people, despite anticipated Chinese mistrust of the "Foreign Devil," which often resulted in stoning or other rough treatment.

Imagine what British photographers of the 1860s—accustomed to the neatly ordered, small-scale British landscape—saw when they focused their lenses in Shanghai, Yokohama, Rangoon, or Shrinagar: huge spaces, disorder, chaos, lush tropical vegetation, exotic people. Initially, they composed, ordered, and applied British aesthetics to their subjects, but Asia was a sweet contagion that invaded soul and photography alike. The British may have ruled these countries and been confident of the rightness of that rule, may have regarded imposed "Britishness" as an improvement, but what shows in these images is a fascinated and often frustrated sense of never quite understanding what Asia was really about yet being spellbound by it nonetheless.

—Pam Roberts, Curator, The Royal Photographic Society, Bath, England

Travelers in Time

Felice Beato (English, 1825–1903)
The Principal Temple at Kamakura, Japan, c. 1863–1868
Albumen print
The Royal Photographic Society, Bath

POMEGRANATE BOX 6099 ROHNERT PARK CA 94927

Travelers in Time

Felice Beato (English, 1825–1903)
Bronze Statue of Dai Bouts, near Kamakura, Japan, c. 1863–1868
Albumen print
The Royal Photographic Society, Bath

POMEGRANATE BOX 6099 ROHNERT PARK CA 94927

Travelers in Time

Samuel Bourne (English, 1834–1912)
and Charles Shepherd (English)
The King of Burmah's Gilded Barge, c. 1876
Albumen print
The Royal Photographic Society, Bath

POMEGRANATE BOX 6099 ROHNERT PARK CA 94927

Travelers in Time

Samuel Bourne (English, 1834–1912)
and Charles Shepherd (English)
*View of Southwest Angle of Pagoda Looking
Toward the Entrance*, c. 1876
Albumen print
The Royal Photographic Society, Bath

POMEGRANATE BOX 6099 ROHNERT PARK CA 94927

Travelers in Time

Samuel Bourne (English, 1834–1912)
The Taj Agra, c. 1864–1870
Albumen print
The Royal Photographic Society, Bath

POMEGRANATE   BOX 6099   ROHNERT PARK CA 94927

Travelers in Time

Samuel Bourne (English, 1834–1912)
Inflated Buffalo Skins (Mussrocks) for Crossing the Beas River,
c. 1864–1870
Albumen print
The Royal Photographic Society, Bath

POMEGRANATE BOX 6099 ROHNERT PARK CA 94927

Travelers in Time

Samuel Bourne (English, 1834–1912)
and Charles Shepherd (English)
War Elephants in Chain Armor from Bikaneer in Rajpootana, c. 1876
Albumen print
The Royal Photographic Society, Bath

POMEGRANATE BOX 6099 ROHNERT PARK CA 94927

Travelers in Time

Samuel Bourne (English, 1834–1912)
Marble Ghat at Rajnuggur, 900 Feet in Length, c. 1864–1870
Albumen print
The Royal Photographic Society, Bath

POMEGRANATE BOX 6099 ROHNERT PARK CA 94927

Travelers in Time

Samuel Bourne (English, 1834–1912)
The Eastern Pagoda from the Entrance, Trichinopoly, 1869
Albumen print
The Royal Photographic Society, Bath

POMEGRANATE BOX 6099 ROHNERT PARK CA 94927

Travelers in Time

Samuel Bourne (English, 1834–1912)
Golden Temple, Umritsur, c. 1864–1870
Albumen print
The Royal Photographic Society, Bath

POMEGRANATE   BOX 6099   ROHNERT PARK CA 94927

Travelers in Time

Samuel Bourne (English, 1834–1912)
Ancient Hindu Temple, Bindrabund, c. 1864–1870
Albumen print
The Royal Photographic Society, Bath

POMEGRANATE BOX 6099 ROHNERT PARK CA 94927

Travelers in Time

Samuel Bourne (English, 1834–1912)
Edge of the Ganges, Varanasi (Benares), c. 1864–1870
Albumen print
The Royal Photographic Society, Bath

POMEGRANATE   BOX 6099   ROHNERT PARK CA 94927

Travelers in Time

Samuel Bourne (English, 1834–1912)
Village of Kibbor, Spiti, c. 1864–1870
Albumen print
The Royal Photographic Society, Bath

POMEGRANATE   BOX 6099   ROHNERT PARK CA 94927

Travelers in Time

Samuel Bourne (English, 1834–1912)
A Toda Mund Village, c. 1864–1870
Albumen print
The Royal Photographic Society, Bath

POMEGRANATE BOX 6099 ROHNERT PARK CA 94927

Travelers in Time

Samuel Bourne (English, 1834–1912)
and Charles Shepherd (English)
Polo Players Who Played Before the Prince of Wales at Calcutta, 1876
Albumen print
The Royal Photographic Society, Bath

POMEGRANATE   BOX 6099   ROHNERT PARK   CA   94927

Travelers in Time

Samuel Bourne (English, 1834–1912)
Mandapum, Showing Three of the Carved Horse Pillars
Albumen print
The Royal Photographic Society, Bath

POMEGRANATE BOX 6099 ROHNERT PARK CA 94927

Travelers in Time

Roger Fenton (English, 1819–1869)
Church of St. Vasili from the Summer Court, Showing the Entrance,
1852
Salted paper print
The Royal Photographic Society, Bath

POMEGRANATE BOX 6099 ROHNERT PARK CA 94927

Travelers in Time

John Thomson (English, 1837–1921)
The Kwo-Tsze-Keen, or National University, Peking, c. 1871–1872
From *Illustrations of China and Its People,* 1873
Collotype
The Royal Photographic Society, Bath

POMEGRANATE   BOX 6099   ROHNERT PARK CA 94927

Travelers in Time

John Thomson (English, 1837–1921)
Peking Observatory, c. 1871–1872
From *Illustrations of China and Its People,* 1873
Collotype
The Royal Photographic Society, Bath

POMEGRANATE BOX 6099 ROHNERT PARK CA 94927

Travelers in Time

John Thomson (English, 1837–1921)
Interior of a Mandarin Dwelling, Peking, c. 1871–1872
From *Illustrations of China and Its People,* 1873
Collotype
The Royal Photographic Society, Bath

POMEGRANATE   BOX 6099   ROHNERT PARK, CA 94927

Travelers in Time

John Thomson (English, 1837–1921)
Yuan Fu Monastery, c. 1870–1871
From *Illustrations of China and Its People*, 1873
Collotype
The Royal Photographic Society, Bath

POMEGRANATE BOX 6099 ROHNERT PARK, CA 94927

Travelers in Time

John Thomson (English, 1837–1921)
Chao-Chow-Fu Bridge
From *Illustrations of China and Its People*, 1873
Collotype
The Royal Photographic Society, Bath

POMEGRANATE   BOX 6099   ROHNERT PARK   CA 94927

Travelers in Time

John Thomson (English, 1837–1921)
Physic Street, Canton
From *Illustrations of China and Its People*, 1873
Collotype
The Royal Photographic Society, Bath

POMEGRANATE   BOX 6099   ROHNERT PARK CA 94927

Travelers in Time

John Thomson (English, 1837–1921)
Buddhist Monks, c. 1870–1871
From *Illustrations of China and Its People*, 1873
Collotype
The Royal Photographic Society, Bath

POMEGRANATE   BOX 6099   ROHNERT PARK CA 94927

Travelers in Time

Captain Linnaeus Tripe (English, 1822–1902)
Side Entrance to the Temple of the Great Bull, Tanjore, c. 1858
Lightly albumenized salt print
The Royal Photographic Society, Bath

POMEGRANATE BOX 6099 ROHNERT PARK CA 94927

Travelers in Time

Walter Bentley Woodbury (English, 1834–1885)
Untitled (temple, Java), c. 1855
Albumen print
The Royal Photographic Society, Bath

POMEGRANATE BOX 6099 ROHNERT PARK CA 94927

Travelers in Time

Walter Bentley Woodbury (English, 1834–1885)
Untitled (portrait of a young man, Java), c. 1855
Albumen print
The Royal Photographic Society, Bath

POMEGRANATE   BOX 6099   ROHNERT PARK CA 94927

Travelers in Time

Samuel Bourne (English, 1834–1912)
and Charles Shepherd (English)
The Great Bell of Mengoon, Said to Weigh 90 Tons, c. 1876
Albumen print
The Royal Photographic Society, Bath

POMEGRANATE   BOX 6099   ROHNERT PARK CA 94927

Travelers in Time

Captain Linnaeus Tripe (English, 1822–1902)
Untitled (Burma), c. 1855
Contemporary print from original paper negative
The Royal Photographic Society, Bath

POMEGRANATE BOX 6099 ROHNERT PARK CA 94927

Travelers in Time

John Thomson (English, 1837–1921)
Stone Animals, Ming Tombs, c. 1871–1872
From *Illustrations of China and Its People*, 1873
Collotype
The Royal Photographic Society, Bath

POMEGRANATE   BOX 6099   ROHNERT PARK CA 94927